Live
so deep
that life
takes your
breath away

mermaid

magic

be mermazing

every day!

Robin Lee

POP PRESS

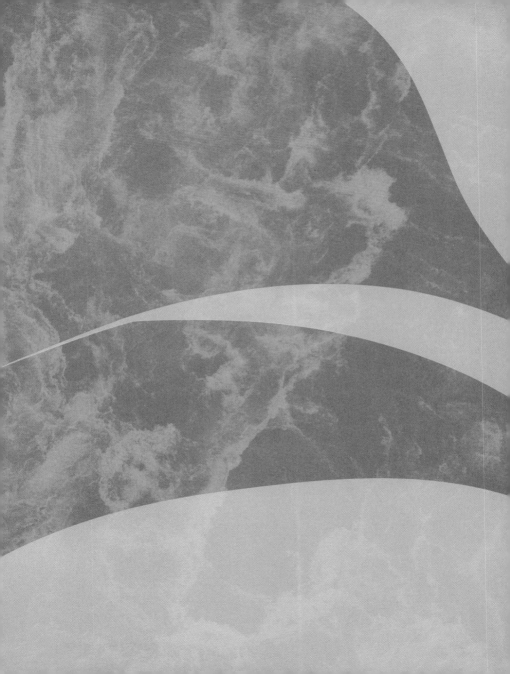

Contents

You Are Mermazing! 9

So Many Sea Babes 12

Find Your Inner Mermaid 38

Kick up Your Sea Adventuress Vibes 75

I Washed up Like This! 99

Making Waves (and Turning Heads) 123

You Are Mermazing!

Hello beautiful!

You hold in your hands a mini guide to mermaiding through life. These pages are a treasure trove of gems and tools to help you embrace your unique inner magic, to believe in yourself no matter how rough the seas and, most importantly, to have fun!

Exploring life as a mermaid is not just about looking pretty and singing really well; she teaches us to be curious about the world around us, to explore the unknown, to dream big and go for what we want. Although mermaids are generally regarded as mythical creatures, you can use their wisdom, confidence and energy to always be your best self and leave a little sparkle wherever you go.

This book is just the beginning of your journey but it's here to inspire you to keep exploring and live out your own powerful ocean-queen dreams.

Now go make some waves!

I didn't choose the mer-life

the mer-life CHOSE ME

So many

sea

babes

What Is a Mermaid?

Tales of the ocean-finned woman started circulating thousands of years ago. We have really made our mark! Sometimes living in castles, sometimes causing mischief (or even disaster...), but always looking for the next adventure, the mermaid is a timeless embodiment of the feminine power that we can all access within ourselves and the power of myth is especially helpful in locating her.

Mermaid Mythology

We can all find ourselves within the archetype of the mermaid. Her representations have been as diverse as Ursula the Sea Witch of *The Little Mermaid* to ancient priestesses of the sea who carried the ability to communicate with whales, dolphins and creatures of all manner. She has been noted in stories in many countries and cultures all over the world.

KICK UP YOUR SEA

adventuress vibes

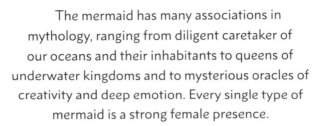

The mermaid has many associations in mythology, ranging from diligent caretaker of our oceans and their inhabitants to queens of underwater kingdoms and to mysterious oracles of creativity and deep emotion. Every single type of mermaid is a strong female presence.

When you close your eyes, take some deep breaths and ask within to reveal yourself in Sea Goddess form, what do you see?

A Sea Goddess thinks for herself, swims for herself and chooses to feel safe and strong in her body daily. What would this feel like for you?

Although there is no scientific proof of the existence of mermaids, they are a really important way for us to understand our own strength and magnificent beauty.

a smooth sea
never made
a skilled
MERMAID

All Sides of the Ocean Goddess

Tales of the mermaid are not always pretty. This is because, for all of us, if we don't make sure to heed the mermaid wisdom of listening to our heart, we can be led astray. Mermaids are women who chart the limitless depths of the ocean. They are also representations of the power of the Feminine to feel deeply, to be led by our heart and to really trust ourselves.

Mermaid Goals

Core traits of the mermaid are related to love and the heart, strength and agility, being cunning and quick to think/move, a joy in the body, and a deep reverence for the natural world and its creatures. She represents the ability of women to conjure up what they desire; to create their own lives, to believe in themselves, to enjoy their bodies and, perhaps most importantly, to be willing to explore the unknown.

SWIM *fast*

WEAR A cro̤Wn

DREAM BIG

Finding Strength in Self-Belief

She is a powerhouse of self-affirmation,
meaning, she doesn't wait around for someone
to tell her that she is strong enough to take on
the tide; she simply does it, because she must.
Exploring everything and staying curious
about life are hallmarks of her
presence within you.

Living a Life of Adventure

Charting the unknown is second nature to
mermaid goddesses, and when we call upon
her within us, she can deeply support us during
challenging times or when making tough decisions.
She asks us to stay true to ourselves, to not be
afraid of the future or the unknown, and
to protect what is important to us.

DIVE
for the
TREASURE
that
YOU seek

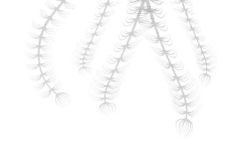

Learning through Life Lessons

The mermaid does have a shadow side, or a side that helps her learn because it shows her where she is still growing her light. This can look like she is giving her heart away too quickly or easily, or not weighing up the possible consequences of decisions, or acting too often on emotion and impulse rather than balancing her choices with a bit of strategy. Each experience with this side makes us stronger.

Finding Balance among the Waves

Mermaid Magic is watery and full of feeling, it is both intense and calm. But it is also unpredictable. To keep life balanced, healthy and full of sparkle, it's important that we remember not to go overboard. This goes hand-in-hand with being a compassionate Sea Babe. The Sirens famously lured men to crash their ships by singing and using their otherworldly beauty for darker purposes. It's best to stay in the light, where we're much more powerful.

She is tossed by the waves, but does not sink

HOLD YOUR HEART AS THOUGH IT WERE A SEASHELL

and listen

to the ocean

within

Connecting to the Energy of Mermaid Magic

It doesn't matter that we live on land, or where we're from, how old we are and what our story is, our inner Mermaid Magic is an energy that all women carry, which connects them to the mysteries of the deep. It is a special connection to the unseen aspects of the world, a deep courage with which to explore life, and a joyful approach to loving and living that we can all learn from and translate into our everyday.

Find

your

inner

mermaid

Mermaids Have More Fin!

Due to the fact that mermaids live underwater, they aren't as attached to ideas such as trying to be perfect, or accumulating a bunch of material things. In fact, what they care most about is generally joy, laughter and a good, solid adventure. Having a bunch of stuff would weigh us down underwater and, frankly, make it really hard to swim!

Remind Yourself That You're SO Loved

In our lives above water, many magical goddesses falsely believe they aren't perfect as they are, or that they need more of something in order to be loveable. Our mermaid mentors show us that, in fact, time is only wasted if we worry about the idea that we're imperfect, and it distracts us from how strong we are, how brave we've been, and how much life there is yet to see.

Mermaid kisses

Starfish wishes

Appreciate Everything in Your World

When we embody the mermaid on earth, we can step most fully into the kind of giddy happiness that we would get from adventuring all day by remembering to be grateful for what we have, and all that life has already given us. Mermaids also know that appreciating the beauty of the world around them is one way in which they begin to see the beauty within themselves as well. That beauty is always reflected back!

Life is short and the ocean is vast

Follow Your Flow

You and I know that the ocean is beautiful,
and living underneath it would be too, but
similarly, we have a whole world above water.
If we appreciate it, we stay present and stop
worrying so much about whether we're enough
of something, we will simply do what feels
good! This is a mermaid principle for life: follow
what feels good.

Appreciate Your Life

So, wherever you are, and however you're feeling, you can activate your inner ocean queen by looking around you and marvelling at the life you have. Find five things (at least) that you are grateful for. Some great examples are: how big your heart is, how strong your body feels, how bright your smile is, and how you have your whole life, still, no matter how old you are, to learn and keep exploring.

Strong Tide?
No Problem

The ocean is always changing. There is a rhythm to the way the tides go in and out, but what it looks like each day is totally different. The ocean simply responds to the weather. Just like life, we can put a plan in place, but leaving room for the unexpected is important! A key to maintaining your mermaid powers is remembering that things outside of you are always going to change. However, the more confident we are in our ability, the less the little things bother us and take us out of our magic.

The
seaweed
is always
greener
in somebody
else's sea

Mermaids don't lose sleep over the opinions of

shrimps

Nurture Your Self-Love Superpowers

Every mermaid must do her best to remember the important art of self-love. This isn't something we feel just when things are going well, when we're proud of ourselves and everything looks great. We are at our most powerful when we are able to love ourselves when we don't feel good, when we've made mistakes and we're not sure what's going to happen next! It's a superpower that takes practice, so remember to be your own biggest supporter.

Be a
mermaid
and
make
wave

Dive Deep
for Positive Thoughts

When you've got a whole ocean to swim across,
it doesn't really help to tell yourself you can't do it,
that you're not strong enough, or that someone
else would be better at it. The same goes for us on
land. If you feel really connected to something,
and you know you have to do it, create it or
otherwise make sure that it happens,
self-love is your best accessory.

Don't Let the Waves Defeat You

Sometimes when we do brave things, like be ourselves completely, other people can be unkind. It's a reminder of what it looks like when someone hasn't learned the Mermaid Arts and doesn't practise self-love. In response to this, we can choose very wisely to demonstrate what it looks like for them by not taking their actions personally. Then we can decide how to tackle that wave in mermaid style.

Laughter is mermaid medicine

Learn Inner Listening

In the land of sea legs, we are taught that our mind is the most important place to get information from. However, the thoughts we carry are not always kind, helpful or supportive. The decision-making process can be pretty disempowering to our Mermaid Magic if we only ever listen to our thoughts. Mermaids are always ruled by the heart. They love deeply, they feel deeply, and they know and understand a lot. Because they live in the mysterious underwater, they can feel things instead of just looking at them and asking questions or drawing conclusions.

Find the Answers within Your Body

If you are feeling overwhelmed or confused about making a decision, try taking a moment to close your eyes, then take a few breaths and let your mind calm down. Try to be away from your phone or your computer or other screens. See how your body feels. You can try inwardly asking a question: does your body contract or feel good when you do this? What messages come to you not from your mind, but from what you feel?

Practise Strong Listening

More often than not, your heart speaks through the language of your body and your feelings. It is much harder to discern what your heart wants, or what is best for your well-being, through thinking alone. So, if you can instead practise listening to what and how you feel, it can activate your Mermaid Magic power of being able to live a life of great adventure that deeply serves you and the people around you. This includes saying 'no' when that's what your body tells you.

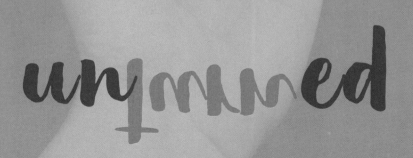

Leave
no seashell
unturned

Let
the sea
set you
FREE

Mirror the Mermaid Magic

It is true that when we are happiest and give ourselves what we need the most, our light shines the brightest and we can offer those we encounter lots of magic simply by mirroring this back to them. When we respect ourselves and our space and feelings, others can respect us, too. A big part of honouring your inner mermaid is inner listening, and the more you practise this, the easier it gets.

Kick up your sea

adventuress
vibes

The Present Moment Is a Big Ocean

Sometimes hard and challenging things happen, and we can get hung up on these events. It can also be easy for us to sometimes get distracted or carried away with thoughts of stormier times. As a mermaid knows best, all this does is distract you from the calm waters at hand. You simply can't enjoy swimming or seeing all that there is to see if you are worrying about a tsunami that isn't on the horizon.

Over-thinking is the downfall of all mermaids. Fun, joy, adventure and bravery are all within our domain, and the biggest way to diminish those feelings is to forget what's right in front of us.

Strong Swimming at Sea

Can you remember to look at life as an adventure? There will certainly be times when your swimming skills are tested, but that is why you are equipped with so much glitter and such a magnificent tail. We, in our deepest mermaid depths, must remember to love all of life, every part of it, for how it grows us and makes us stronger. The stronger we become, the further out we can venture to see things that many others might not get to see in their lives! When we are brave, we are always rewarded in this way.

Live
by the sea
Love
by the Moon

Shoot for the Stars

Mermaids love to make art of all kinds and see all that there is to see. Whether it is a form of creative expression such as singing, dancing, writing, acting, sculpting, painting and beyond, or if your art is maths and science and geology, every mermaid knows that the true path to happiness is letting these things flow free to be explored! She proudly owns who she is and all of her talents, letting people see her shine.

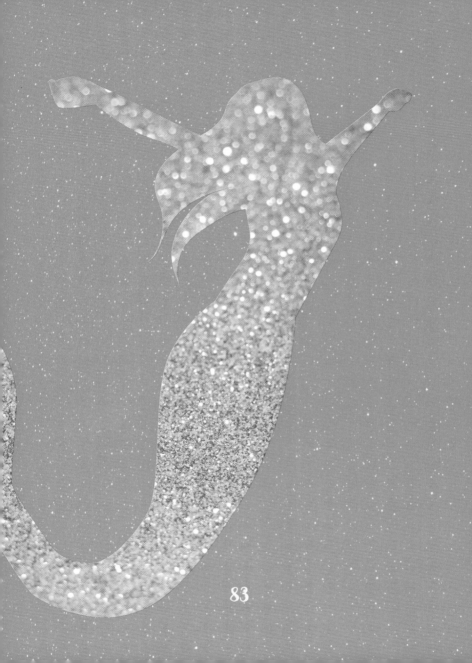

My home is
the open
sea, where the

stars burn

brighter and

my soul is

FREE

Protect Your Magic

Being your own biggest supporter is a mermaid trait that should not be shaken. A mermaid knows that when she steps boldly into being herself and finds the happiness that it brings, other people might have a thing or two to say about it. The ocean, just like the world itself, is vast. Those who cannot handle your shine needn't be part of your adventure, and there is plenty of room for every mermaid to take up her own space in the spotlight. A mermaid doesn't turn off the glimmer of her scales or pretend she doesn't have powers, she needs them to survive! And so do you.

Saltwater

cures all

wounds

Trust Your Tail!

Water has symbolically been associated with dreams, intuition and the things that we can't explain but that we feel deeply. As a mermaid, and a goddess who hails from such a space, it would be totally out of character for us not to pay attention to our intuition, not to notice our dreams, and not to give weight to the things that might not have rational explanations. Women are full of mysterious superpowers. One of these, in particular, is our ability to simply know things about other people or situations, or even places, by the gut feeling we often have when we are near them.

If there's a will,

there's

a wave

Your Ocean GPS

We can learn to use these feelings as a sort of GPS for how we move through the world. Because mermaids are very heart-centred people, it becomes really important to make sure that we are also good at having boundaries. This means saying 'no' when necessary and generally making sure we stand up for ourselves. If something doesn't feel quite right to us, it probably isn't! Don't be afraid to ask for what you need, to ask for a change or otherwise speak your truth.

'I must be a mermaid. I have no fear of depths, and a great fear of shallow living.'

ANAÏS NIN

Finding Quiet in the Maelstrom of Our Minds

To activate our intuition most effectively,
it's important that we take some quiet time in the
morning and at night to calm our bodies and minds,
by taking deep breaths and even closing our eyes.
This way, our thoughts can slow down enough so
that we can hear that smart voice underneath.
Even if this is a hard habit for you to start, after
doing it just a few times it is easy to see how much
better you feel. Let that be your motivation
to keep doing it!

I washed up like this!

Love Your Body

The strength of your body and how it can carry you to see incredible sights, have wonderful experiences and have the energy to keep chasing your dreams, is a magnificent gift. In the non-mermaid world, we are often told that the value of our beautiful bodies comes from what they look like. But the truth is, it doesn't matter what a body looks like, it matters how it feels! The best way to make sure your body feels amazing to you is to really be alive in it. To enjoy it. To love it. To feel your strength in it!

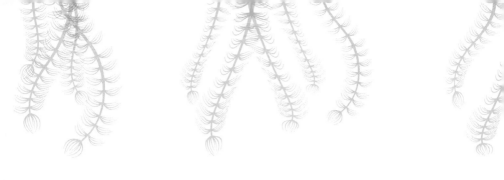

Resting and Playing

Make time each day to engage in playful movement, even if it's just a few minutes of dancing, stretching or rolling onto your yoga mat and seeing what feels good. Our bodies go through a lot of stress each day and sometimes there is pressure to look or be a certain way. It can be a huge relief to simply let your body be, and to let it tell you what it needs, including rest! Eating, moving and resting in ways that make you feel good are extremely important mermaid skills.

You

Siren

You!

Swim to your ocean music

Express Yourself

Let's face it, being a Sea Goddess and a Magical
Mermaid isn't always welcomed by everyone! There
are lots of different fish in the sea, as we know.
Consistently seeking out joy and adventure in life in
ways that feel good to us, as well as really loving our
bodies and supporting ourselves, can sometimes
challenge messages that we get as girls and women
about who we're supposed to be, according to
someone else!

Let Your Uniqueness Lure in Others

It's not very exciting to live by someone else's
standards and it takes us away from all of the magic
we've talked about so far. Although we might feel
different sometimes, it's important to remember
that those differences can be an invitation to others
to shine their light, too. Seeing a mermaid on land
in her full glory is a very special experience. When
we see people who really love themselves and
accept themselves, it's a joy to be around them.
And the more you let your uniqueness be seen,
the easier it is to find the other mermaids!

Mermaid Style: Dress for the High Seas

It can be a lot of fun to start to bring your mermaid energy into your everyday life by infusing the way you dress with a touch of magic. Getting dressed should really be about us and what makes us happy and feel totally expressed, so adding a solid dose of Sea Babe can't do any harm. Read on for some easy ways to play with your Mermaid Magic that don't need to be totally obvious to other people, unless you want them to be!

Be a
mermaid
in an
ocean full
of fish

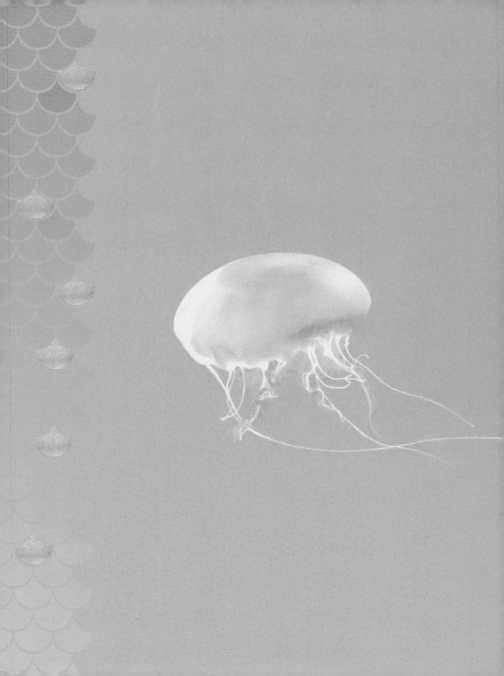

Fill Your Wardrobe with Sparkle and Flow

Just as the ocean radiates under the moonlight and the sand glitters with the sun, we can reflect our ocean vibes out into the world by playing with a little sparkle. It doesn't have to be anything too outrageous, even a touch will do! Watery fabrics and materials with a silky touch are great reminders of feeling good in our bodies, as well as the fluid nature of the world of water that we come from. Silk, satin and other soft or flowing things can be a great way to weave a little ocean goddess into your day.

The greatest adventure you will ever go on

is becoming

who you

really are

inside

Find Sea Energy in Colour

Sea foam, sky and sea grass can all be brought to life in our realms, no matter how drab the surroundings appear to be. Bring these colours into your wardrobe for a dose of soothing, calming sea energy. Colour has a lot of power to shift our moods and feelings, and ocean tones are very relaxing!

Adorn Your Vessel

All goddesses deserve to be adorned in the way that they see fit. For some it might be big statement jewellery and elaborate colours; for others it might be small accents that make you feel beautiful. Explore what feels right for you, fun for you and, more importantly, what will express a part of who you are!

Mermaid hair

Don't care

The best
wave of
your life

is still

out there

Making Waves
(and Turning Heads)

The greatest adventure we will ever go on is becoming who we really are inside. Your confidence will take you to incredible places, your strength and sense of adventure will keep you ready for anything and your self-love will inspire others, too.

But remember, when we become really bright and unafraid it can sometimes ruffle the scales of other sea-dwellers. Don't let this deter you from continuing to seek the treasures of your life. A mermaid can't slow down for those who don't believe in her ability to swim. If you keep shining, the ones who understand you will always find you.

Champion your own gloriousness and the diversity of others and, if you can, remember that everyone is doing their best in this big ocean, and you'll be embodying your magic with grace.

May you valiantly brave the tides and let your gorgeous goddess ocean glory be witnessed by all!

ALWAYS
BE
YOURSELF

Unless you can
be a mermaid

10 9 8 7 6 5 4 3 2 1

Pop Press, an imprint of Ebury Publishing,
20 Vauxhall Bridge Road,
London, SW1V 2SA

Pop Press is part of the Penguin Random
House group of companies whose
addresses can be found at global.
penguinrandomhouse.com

Penguin
Random House
UK

First published by Pop Press in 2018

www.penguin.co.uk

A CIP catalogue record for this book is
available from the British Library

ISBN 9781785038747

Printed and bound in China by Toppan
Leefung

MIX
Paper from
responsible sources
FSC   FSC® C018179
www.fsc.org

Penguin Random House is committed
to a sustainable future for our business,
our readers and our planet. This book
is made from Forest Stewardship
Council® certified paper.

Text by Robin Lee ©POP PRESS

Robin Lee has asserted her right to be
identified as the author of this Work in
accordance with the Copyright, Designs
and Patents Act 1988

Design and illustrations: maru studio

Photos © Unsplash
p.1 Jared Poledna; p.2-3, 24, 61, 90 Jeremy
Bishop; p.2-3, 13, 38-39, 75, 86, 96, 98,
122 [star background] Ohmky; p.4, 58
Nathan Roser; p.10 Zen Photographer;
p.10 Patrick Brinksma, p.20, 116 Shifaaz
Shamoon; p.26, 31 Biel Morro; p.29, 112
Scott Webb; p.33, 44, 80 Nathan Dumlao;
p.34, 64 Amy; p.36 Christoffer Engstrom;
p.43, 66, 69 Sime Basioli; p.46 Haythem
Gataa; p.48 Greg Becker; p.51 Li Yang;
p.53 Wembley; p.54 Vlad Tchompalov;
p.56, 70 Yannis Papanastasopoulos; p.62,
111 Jordan Whitfield; p.72 Joshua Rawson
Harris; p.79 Nadia Jamnik; p.82 Jeremy
Perkins; p.85 Shoot n design; p.88 Toa
Heftiba; p.93 Joshua Reddekopp; p. 94
Mikita Amialkovic; p.96, 121 Tim Marshall;
p.103 Andreas Fidler; p.104 Ricardo Gomez
Angel; p.106 Samuel Scrimshaw; p.109
Melissa Logan; p.114 Benjamin Voros; p.119
Camila Cordeiro; p.124 Nsey Benajah; p.126
freestock org

Extras illustrations:
Illustrations © Adobe Stock: cover [holographic] © Anja Kaiser; cover [bubbles], p. 6, 12, 38, 74, 98 [bubbles] © mything; p.2, 7,
14-15, 40-41, 76-77, 83, 100, 112-113, 122-123 [silver bckg] © 4 Girls 1 Boy; p.2 [hair], p4-5 © prochkailo; p.14-15 © mikabesfamilnaya;
p.18-19 [pattern in tails] © maritime_m; p.23 © sezamvlr; p.31 [head only];© Anastasia; p.38-39 [dolphins], 43, 46-47, 62-63, 66-67
[tail and jellyfish], 70-71 [fish, seaweeds, dolphins] 73 [fish], 80-81, 96, 99, 106-107 [tail, hair], 109 [tail], 116, 126-127 [tail, shellfish]
© Gluiki; p.40-41 © CNuisin; p.70 [head], 109 [hair] © MicroOne; p.76-77 © blumer1979, p.100-101 © newrossosh

Illustrations by Julie Binchet: p.8-9 [seahorse, stars]; seaweed on pages 16, 21, 30-32, 36-37, 42, 45, 50-51, 56-57, 59, 65, 73, 78,
86-87, 96-97, 102, 105, 116-117; coral on pages p.25, 49, 68, 110; hair on pages 118-119